AUSSIE CEREAL CLASSICS

BOOK ONE

Welcome to the first edition in this series, all about Aussie cereal premiums of the 1960s and '70s.

It was in the psychedelic late '60s that pop culture really exploded. 1967–71 was a great time to be a young kid. It was the 'groovy' era of Bubblegum music, made especially for us (although it had inappropriately adult overtones at times).

On TV we had *Batman*, *Lost in Space*, *The Monkees*, *Cattanooga Cats*, *Banana Splits* (with *Danger Island*), *Wacky Races*, *Skippy*, *HR Pufnstuf*, *F Troop*, *Get Smart* and much more. No colour, but we got that elsewhere.

The cinema brought us *Jungle Book*, *Chitty Chitty Bang Bang*, *The Love Bug*, *The Aristocats*, *Willy Wonka and the Chocolate Factory*, *Bedknobs and Broomsticks*.

At the shops there were bubblegum cards with monsters in hot rods, an endless new variety of fizzy drinks, Glugs, Razzes, Flintstones bottles, chocolate bars and snacks with cartoon stickers in them... Hot Wheels, Kooky Spooky ghost puppets that glowed in the dark... mindbending comics about the Silver Surfer, Dr Strange and Nick Fury. Non-stop Casper, Hot Stuff, Little Dot, Richie Rich...

And those cereal boxes. It seemed there was always some colourful new set to collect – because there was. It was the brilliant box art that sold us on the premiums within.

Most of these were produced by the R&L company in Melbourne, although we had no idea of that at the time.

We'd cut out the panels, display them on our shelves... then throw them out to make room when the next, 'better' thing came along.

Despite millions of boxes being produced, only a handful of the panels are still in existence today. Fortunately, over many years of collecting, I've been able to get examples of many of them.

They've usually been damaged or incomplete. Some survived only because they were used for scrawling notes on their backs, or as backing for scrapbooks, recipes or jigsaws. I've managed to digitally restore many of them, obsessively putting hundreds of hours into the task. It takes all kinds, right?

My focus is on preserving these rare, ephemeral examples of Aussie pop-culture that were never intended to last beyond a two-month sales cycle.

In this first edition, I'm featuring a gallery of our favourite vintage cartoon-style panels. There are, of course, some panels I don't have at all. This is why Swinging Pets, Stretch Pets, Kiddy Keys or Crazy Insects (for example) don't appear here. But by far the majority of our favourites are present.

Future editions will showcase the panels from transport, animal and historical series, as well as the various oddities that were printed all those decades ago.

There will also be at least two editions of Aussie Cereal Classics that will highlight the plastic premiums themselves. These will give overviews and impressions of the sets, accompanied by actual-size colour photos of each premium.

I'll provide details on the colours they came in, and which items are particularly rare.

Australian Cereal Classics Book 1, June 2021. LIMITED 1st PRINTING.
Restoration, compilation and written content ©2021 Peter Markmann.

ケロッグをたべて ゆかいな宇宙人を 集めよう!!

これはユカイだ！おもしろい！
ケロッグの箱を、あけてびっくり！見てびっくり！いままで、オモチャ屋さんに売っていなかった、ゆかいな宇宙人が、どの箱にも1個ずつ、はいっています。かたちはみんなで8種類！色は4色！さあ、ケロッグをたべて、オマケのかわいい宇宙人を集めましょう！みーんな集めて、ユカイに遊びましょう！

お母さまへ・・・・お子さまは遊びの天才。ケロッグのゆかいな宇宙人から、いろいろな遊びを発見し、宇宙への夢を大きく育てるでしょう。

ケロッグ・コーンフロスト、フルーツポンの箱には、上の宇宙パノラマの切りぬきがついています。こんどはケロッグ・コーンフロスト、フルーツポンを買って、宇宙パノラマと宇宙人で、もっとゆかいに遊びましょう。

Kellogg's STRAWBERRY POPS CRATER CRITTERS

THERE'S ONE INSIDE THIS PACKET—COLLECT ALL EIGHT!!

PANEL No. 1

Here are the cutest creatures you have ever collected—Kellogg's "Crater Critters". Normally they live way down in the deepest craters on a far-off planet. They are shy little people that's why we hardly ever see them. There are 8 "Crater Critters" to collect. You'll find them in every large packet of Kellogg's Corn Flakes and O.K's. Collect them all and make them your friends, their names are:—

KINGLY CRITTER: is the happy King of all the Crater Critters. That's why he wears a crown. **CLEVER CRITTER:** Clever does all sorts of smart tricks. He loves to balance on one foot and show off. **CRAWLY CRITTER:** Crawly likes to pretend to frighten everyone by pulling horrible faces, but he doesn't mean any harm. **CURLY CRITTER:** Curly doesn't talk very much, but he loves to listen. That's why his ears are so large. **CRANKY CRITTER:** Cranky likes to argue. He always looks a bit grumpy. **CREEPY CRITTER:** Creepy looks awful, but he's really very nice. **KINDLY CRITTER:** Kindly loves everyone. He never does anything naughty or unkind. **KOOKY CRITTER:** Kooky is always playing crazy tricks. Sometimes you don't know if he's upside-down or right-way-up.

By the way, don't miss collecting the story of "The Planets" on the back of every 8 oz. size packet of Kellogg's Corn Flakes.

Kellogg's COCO POPS Noodle Nodders

How about these for real living-animal fun ! Put them in a breeze, fan them, or blow on them, and they *all* move their heads — that's why they are called 'Noodle Nodders.' There are 8 different 'Noodle Nodders' to collect. You'll find one in every packet of Kellogg's Coco Pops,* Sugar Frosties,* Honey Smacks* and Froot Loops.*

Collect them all, call them by their names, and they will noodle nod for you.

* Registered Trade Marks

CRAZY CAMEL TRAIN

PANEL No. 2

Here's the wackiest train-of-the-desert you've ever seen—Kellogg's Crazy Camel Train. You can imagine yourself on Economy Class Camel, Camel First Class, or driving the Camel Engine across the Sahara. There are 8 cute 'n crazy plastic models for you to collect. And there's 6 colourful desert railway 'cut-outs' for you to make up and complete a whole desert railway system! You'll find your lovable plastic desert-characters in every large packet of Kellogg's Corn Flakes and OK's. · Add to your own desert world by collecting the pictures and story of 'Desert Dwellers' on the back of every packet of Kellogg's 8 oz Corn Flakes.

HOW TO MAKE YOUR RAILWAY BRIDGE.

Cut around heavy outlines. All broken lines fold DOWN. All dotted lines fold UP. Join tab, A to B, C to D, E to F, G to H, I to J, and K to L. Assemble as shown in diagram.

*Registered Trade Mark

CRAZY CAMEL TRAIN

PANEL No. 2

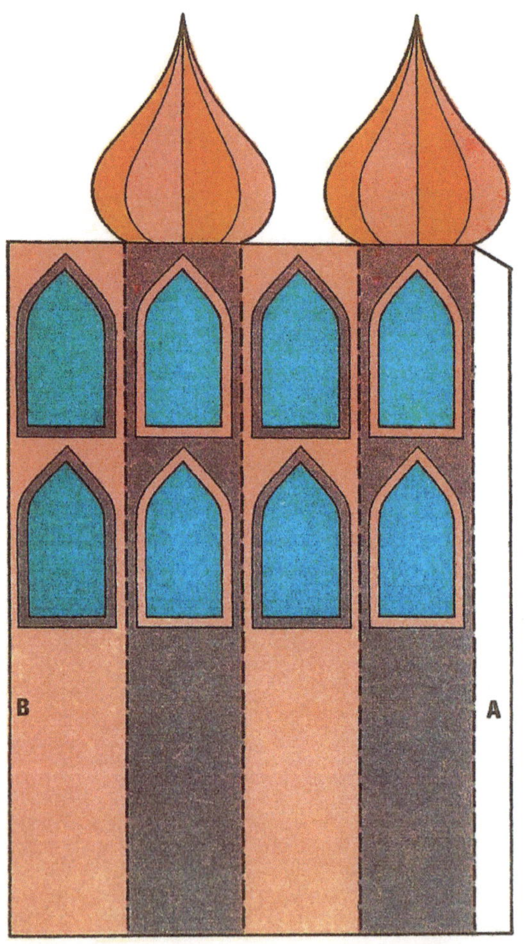

Here's the wackiest train-of-the-desert you've ever seen—Kellogg's Crazy Camel Train. You can imagine yourself on Economy Class Camel, Camel First Class, or driving the Camel Engine across the Sahara. There are 8 cute 'n crazy plastic models for you to collect. And there's 6 colourful desert railway 'cut-outs' for you to make up and complete a whole desert railway system! You'll find your lovable plastic desert-characters in every large packet of Kellogg's Corn Flakes and OK's.* Add to your own desert world by collecting the pictures and story of 'Desert Dwellers' on the back of every packet of Kellogg's 8 oz Corn Flakes.

HOW TO MAKE YOUR RAILWAY WATCH TOWER. Score broken lines, cut around heavy outlines. All broken lines fold DOWN. Join tabs A, B and C to D. Glue tower to inside wall as shown in diagram.

*Registered Trade Mark

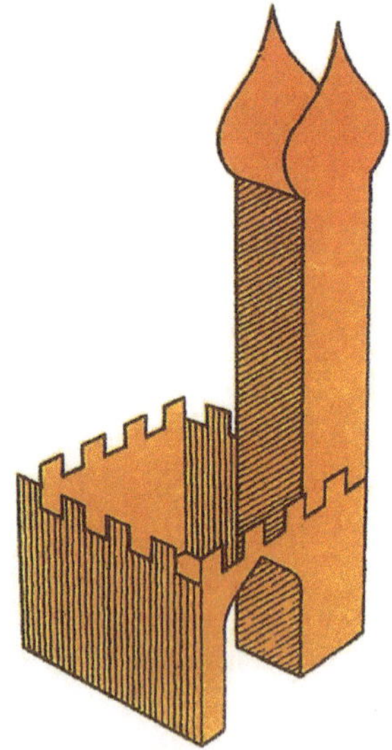

Kellogg's CORN FLAKES | CRAZY CAMEL TRAIN

PANEL No. 3

Here's the wackiest train-of-the-desert you've ever seen—Kellogg's Crazy Camel Train. You can imagine yourself on Economy Class Camel, Camel First Class, or driving the Camel Engine across the Sahara. There are 8 cute 'n crazy plastic models for you to collect. And there's 6 colourful desert railway 'cut-outs' for you to make up and complete a whole desert railway system! You'll find your lovable plastic desert-characters in every large packet of Kellogg's Corn Flakes and OK's. * Add to your own desert world by collecting the pictures and story of 'Desert Dwellers' on the back of every packet of Kellogg's 8 oz Corn Flakes.

HOW TO MAKE YOUR WATER TANK. Score broken lines. Cut around heavy outlines. All broken lines fold DOWN. Join tab A to B. Glue tabs C.D.E. and F *inside* the tank shape, as shown in diagram.

*Registered Trade Mark

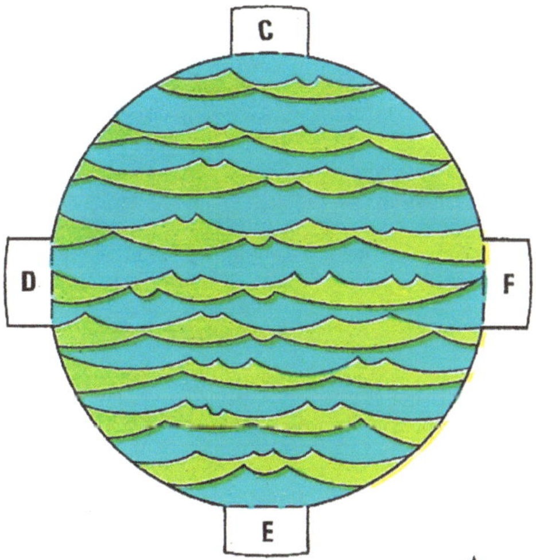

CRAZY CAMEL TRAIN

PANEL No. 6

Here's the wackiest train-of-the-desert you've ever seen—Kellogg's Crazy Camel Train. You can imagine yourself on Economy Class Camel, Camel First Class, or driving the Camel Engine across the Sahara. There are 8 cute 'n crazy plastic models for you to collect. And there's 6 colourful desert railway 'cut-outs' for you to make up and complete a whole desert railway system. You'll find your lovable plastic desert-characters in every large packet of Kellogg's Corn Flakes and OK's . Add to your own desert world by collecting the pictures and story of 'Desert Dwellers' on the back of every packet of Kellogg's 8 oz Corn Flakes.

HOW TO MAKE YOUR EL PYRAMID COFFEE SHOPPE. Score broken and dotted lines. Cut around heavy outlines. All broken lines fold DOWN All dotted lines fold UP Join tab, A to B, C to D, and E to F. Assemble as shown in diagram.

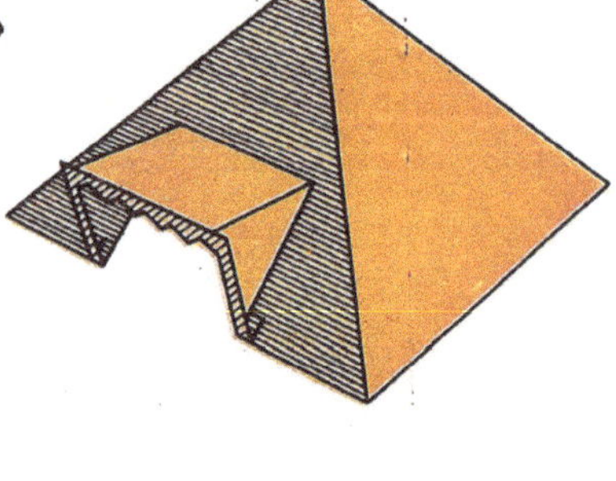

8 different Camel Train Figures to collect...ONE FREE in each specially-marked Sugar Smacks package...get 'em all!

HERE'S HOW TO PUT TOGETHER THE FIGURE YOU GET FREE IN THIS PACKAGE:

ALL FIGURES:

Carefully separate figure sections from frame (as shown). Trim off any excess plastic so parts fit together properly.

ALL CAMELS:

Press side of Camel together, fitting prong on one side into corresponding hole in opposite. (Camels with wheels: slide axles into holes in base and slip on wheels. Insert hooks for connecting Camel to another train section into slots at each end of base.)

ENGINE:

Put together in same manner as you do a Camel with wheels. (See Camel instructions at left.)

CAMEL CANOPY*:

Fit prongs in one side of Canopy into corresponding holes in opposite side and press together.

MONKEY BED*:

Fit prong in one side of Bed in corresponding hole in opposite side and press together.

SETTING FIGURES ON CAMELS:

Set Camel Canopy*, Monkey Bed*, and Monkey Figures on Camels as shown on Camel Train pictured above. Monkey Figures with flag and banana stand alone as shown. Ladder leans against Camel without wheels.

*NOTE: Camel Canopy and Monkey Bed fit on Camels you get FREE in other Kellogg's Sugar Smacks packages.

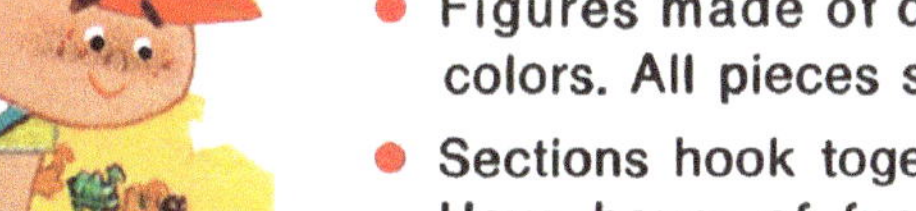

- Figures made of durable plastic in assorted, bright colors. All pieces snap together—nothing to glue.

- Sections hook together like a real train...wheels turn. Have hours of fun pulling your Camel Train through a "make-believe" desert.

Kellogg's CORN FLAKES

NEP-TUNE and his SWITCHED·ON·SEAWEEDERS

NEP-TUNE
He's the groovy daddy of them all. He can conduct anything from cool jazz to thundering symphonies.

HAPPY HIPPY SEA HORSE He loves the off-beat, and is at his best with the cool Latin sambas and rumbas.

BUBBLES BLOWFISH
She's a girl with a lot of talent and she blows a slinky horn that wails out the deep-sea blues.

MIKE MER-KID
The babe with the harmonica rattles up and down the scales like a veteran.

OCTOPUSSY HEP-CAT
He's a cool swingin' cat who improvises up and down on his vibrating xylophone.

TWANGY TURTLE
He's another Dixieland cat who sings as he plays on his twanging sea shell guitar.

COOL CONNIE CORAL
She's the 'dolly' of the deep. The go-go-girl who keeps the band swinging.

SLUGSY SEA SHELL
He loves the slugging downbeat and really goes to town with the brass trio.

Here's a real cool swinging group for you to collect. Kellogg's Nep-Tune and his Switched-on-Seaweeders. There are 15 of these crazy under-sea musicians in Nep-Tune's band. You can collect all 15, or you can collect 3 and make a trio, 4 and make a quartette; 5 and make a quintette etc. Put your groups in front of your two background panels and join Nep-Tune in conducting your own musical score. You'll find these deep-sea musicians in every large packet of Kellogg's Corn Flakes and OK's*. And don't miss the exciting colourful story of 'Man Under Sea' on the back of every packet of Kellogg's 8 oz. Corn Flakes.

How to assemble your background panels
Cut around heavy black line. Glue tab A and tab B *behind* Panel No. 2, as shown in diagram.   *Registered Trade Mark

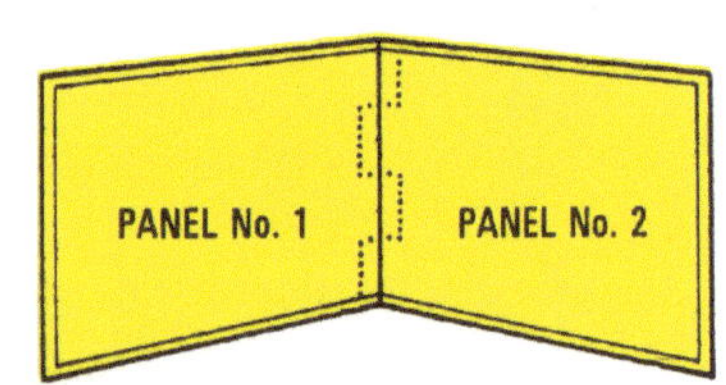

NEP-TUNE
He's the groovy daddy of them all. He can conduct anything from cool jazz to thundering symphonies.

SAXY SALMON
He blows a smooth-as-silk saxophone and is at his best with cool deep-sea music.

HARPY HARP
At the flick of a feeler he becomes the only self-harping harp in the sea–music world.

FAB CRAB
He goes wild on his deep toned shell bass fiddle. He plays fast, but always right on the beat.

SYNCOPATING SEA HORSE He blows a cool wailing trumpet and prefers Dixieland jazz to the classics.

PLONKY PIANO
The deep blue chords come naturally to Plonky. He loves playing all around the original melody.

TOM TOM TURTLE
He's the booming drum in the band, helped by his small enthusiastic friend, Tiny Tim Turtle.

FRANTIC FANNY FANTAIL She really prefers Opera, and can hit top C with ease. She also shakes a mean hip.

Here's a real cool swinging group for you to collect.
Kellogg's Nep-Tune and his Switched-on-Seaweeders. There are 15 of these crazy under-sea musicians in Nep-Tune's band. You can collect all 15, or you can collect 3 and make a trio, 4 and make a quartette; 5 and make a quintette etc. Put your groups in front of your two background panels and join Nep-Tune in conducting your own musical score. You'll find these deep-sea musicians in every large packet of Kellogg's Corn Flakes and OK's*. And don't miss the exciting colourful story of 'Man Under Sea' on the back of every packet of Kellogg's 8 oz. Corn Flakes.

How to assemble your background panels
Cut around heavy black line. Glue tab C and tab D *behind* Panel No. 1, as shown in diagram.   *Registered Trade Mark

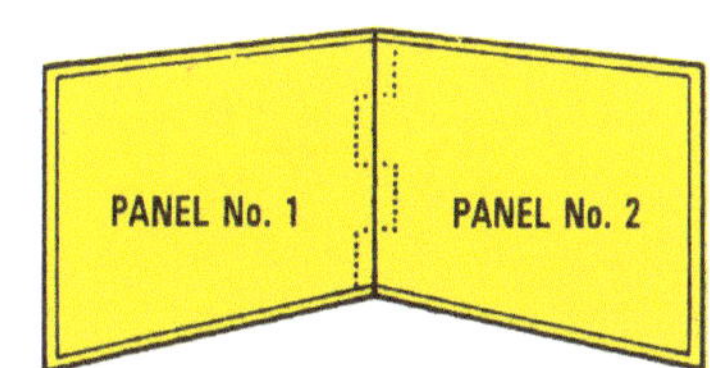

14

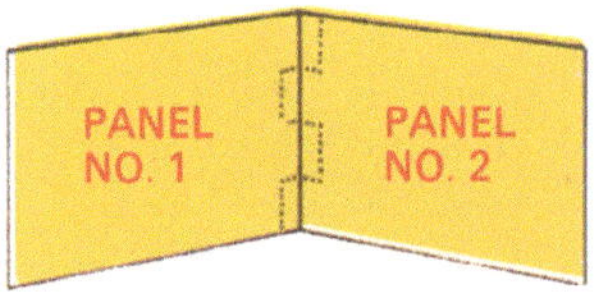

Only Kellogg's could bring you this fantastic collection of way-out fun creatures called 'The Fringies'. These mystical little people live beyond-the-fringe of outer space and they have powers to help those who are always kind to 'littlies.' Collect them all. Thread them on a string and wear them.

Tie them on to your belt, coat lapel, or stand them on your bedroom shelf.
There are 15 *different* "Fringies" to collect. You'll find them in every packet of Kellogg's Rice Chex, Corn Chex, Wheat Flakes, Puffed Wheat, and OK's.* Call them by name and make them your friends.

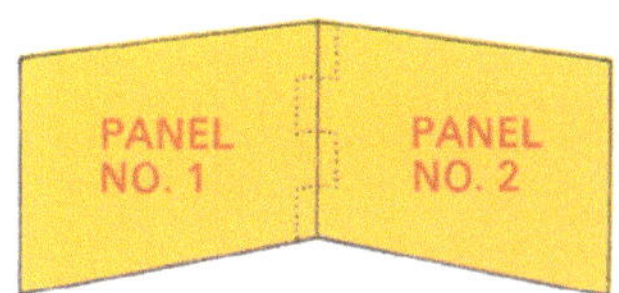

Paddy Paint Brush · Georgie Grubbing Axe · Oliver Oil-Can · Cuthbert Chopper · Marty Monkey-wrench · Charlie Chisel · Muggsie Mallet · Henry Handbrace

Did you ever see such building kooks? Here are the craziest beaky-building-birds you've ever collected! Kellogg's "Tooly Birds" are the workers of a fantasy bird family. They use their beaks to chisel, hammer, saw, and drill. There are 16 different "Tooly Birds" for you to collect. You'll find them in every packet of Kellogg's Corn Flakes and OK's.*

How to assemble your colourful background panels: Cut around heavy black line. Glue tab A and tab C *behind* Panel No. 2, as shown in diagram.

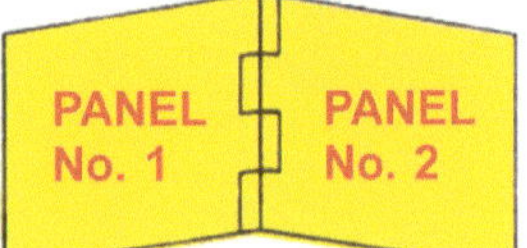

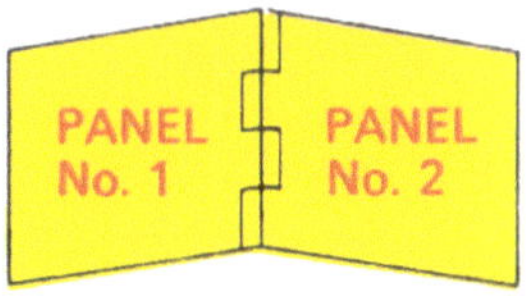

VEGETABLE SPORTS!

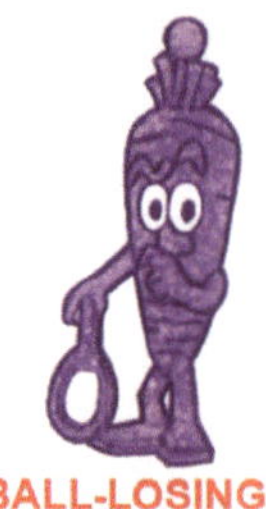

You've never seen such a team of sporting weirdies as Kellogg's 'Vegetable Sports!' Every year they hold their own Olympic Games. Nobody wins of course, and although some of them may look cross, they are all good friends.

There are 8 *different* 'Vegetable Sports' for you to collect. Call them by name—see which one is best in *your* team. You'll find these zany characters in every packet of Kellogg's Coco Pops,* Sugar Frosties,* Honey Smacks,* and Froot Loops.*

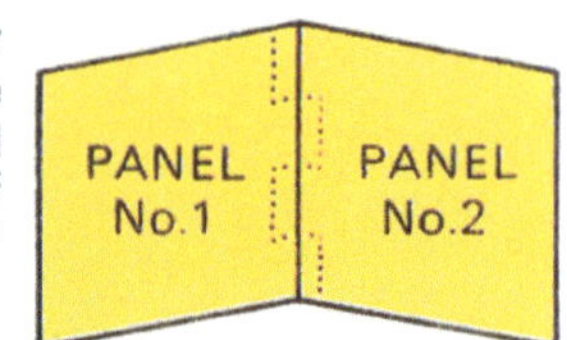

VEGETABLE SPORTS!

RUNNER BEAN **SKATER ONION** **SPOONY BEAN** **SPUDSY BOXER** **STILTY CARROT** **STARTER MUSHROOM** **SCOOTY SHALLOT** **BALL-LOSING CARROT**

You've never seen such a team of sporting weirdies as Kellogg's 'Vegetable Sports'! Every year they hold their own Olympic Games. Nobody wins of course, and although some of them may look cross, they are all good friends.

There are 8 *different* 'Vegetable Sports' for you to collect. Call them by name—see which one is best in *your* team. You'll find these zany characters in every packet of Kellogg's Coco Pops,* Sugar Frosties,* Honey Smacks,* and Froot Loops.*

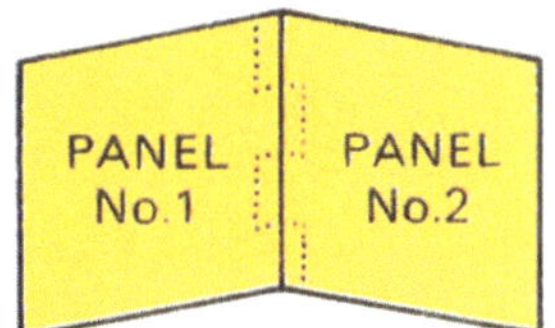

Kellogg's COCO POPS ZOO CHOO TRAIN

Here's the kookiest fun choo-choo you have ever collected – Kellogg's "Zoo Choo Train". From Joe-Jumbo-Engine to Willie-Oil-Whale, Harry Hippo Tanker, and Minnie-bulk-Milk, you'll love collecting them all, and making up your own train.

There are 10 way-out creatures for you to collect! You'll find them in every packet of Kellogg's Coco Pops,* Sugar Frosties,* Froot Loops,* Honey Smacks,* and Ricicles.* Collect them all, and chug-chug-chug them around on your bedside table or bookshelf.

COLLECT THEM ALL

Round and round they go in lunar orbit, in their rockets and their flying saucers, the mad, crazy Kellogg's "Astro-nits". With retro-rockets firing they zoom into earth orbit to land on *your* breakfast table. So you can recognize them, we have stamped a dotty name on every one of them.

There are TWENTY "Astro-nits" for you to collect! And would you believe it, there are TWO "Astro-nits" in EVERY packet of Kellogg's Coco Pops,* Frosties,* Honey Smacks,* Froot Loops,* Ricicles,* Lettabits,* and Strawberry Pops*. Wow! What a crazy mob to play with, and keep on your bedroom shelf.

* Registered Trade Marks

CORNY CANINES

   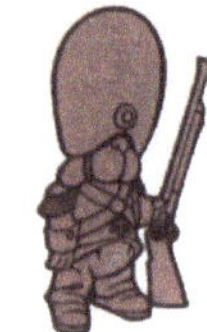    

HARRY HUNTER
the gundog pretends to be a crack shot! He looks rather scarey, but when nobody's looking he fires his gun into the air to frighten nasty crows away.

BRAVE BILLY
the boxer dog, loves to spar around the ring with his friends. He pulls fierce faces and g-r-o-w-l-s, but never harms anyone.

RACING ROGER
the jockey dog, thinks he is king of the track. He saddles up his horse, and races round and round the track — but never wins anything.

GEORGE GRENADIER
the guard dog, means it when he hollers "Halt who goes there?" But with his hat hiding his eyes —very often there's nobody there!

CLAUDE CLIMBER
the guide dog, loves to yodel his way up big snowy mountains. Sometimes he pretends to fall, but he's surefooted and never loses his way.

MANUEL MEX
the singing dog is naughty. He hates to work. He would rather sit in the sun, strum a guitar and sing folk songs all day—all out of tune!

SAMMY SHEPHERD
the sheep dog, looks like a real sad-sam. He's a bit grumpy, but he's really kind and tramps around all day to keep his sheep from straying.

COCKER COP
is a busy police dog. He can see through all his friend's tricks. He's stern, but fair, and he'll give you a ticket if you do anything naughty, or are unkind.

Here's the greatest collection of loveable doggie-scallywags you have ever seen! All of them live together in Kellogg's fantastic doggie-land village. They all love to dress up, and they work hard at doing their own thing.

There are 8 kooky "Corny Canines" for you to collect. You'll find one of them in every large packet of Kellogg's Corn Flakes. And don't miss the "Dotty Dog" colour-ins on the back of every packet of Kellogg's 8oz Corn Flakes!

PANEL NO. 1.

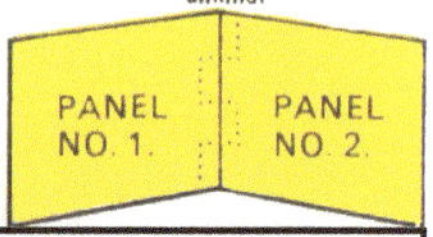

PANEL NO. 1.   PANEL NO. 2.

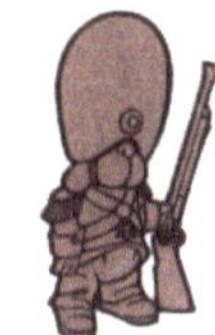

HARRY HUNTER the gundog pretends to be a crack shot! He looks rather scarey, but when nobody's looking he fires his gun into the air to frighten nasty crows away.

BRAVE BILLY the boxer dog, loves to spar around the ring with his friends. He pulls fierce faces and g-r-o-w-l-s, but never harms anyone.

RACING ROGER the jockey dog, thinks he is king of the track. He saddles up his horse, and races round and round the track — but never wins anything.

GEORGE GRENADIER the guard dog, means it when he hollers "Halt who goes there?" But with his hat hiding his eyes —very often there's nobody there!

CLAUDE CLIMBER the guide dog, loves to yodel his way up big snowy mountains. Sometimes he pretends to fall, but he's surefooted and never loses his way.

MANUEL MEX the singing dog is naughty. He hates to work. He would rather sit in the sun, strum a guitar and sing folk songs all day—all out of tune!

SAMMY SHEPHERD the sheep dog, looks like a real sad-sam. He's a bit grumpy, but he's really kind and tramps around all day to keep his sheep from straying.

COCKER COP is a busy police dog. He can see through all his friend's tricks. He's stern, but fair, and he'll give you a ticket if you do anything naughty, or are unkind.

Here's the greatest collection of loveable doggie-scallywags you have ever seen! All of them live together in Kellogg's fantastic doggie-land village. They all love to dress up, and they work hard at doing their own thing.

There are 8 kooky "Corny Canines" for you to collect. You'll find one of them in every large packet of Kellogg's Corn Flakes. And don't miss the "Dotty Dog" colour-ins on the back of every packet of Kellogg's 8oz Corn Flakes! **PANEL NO. 2.**

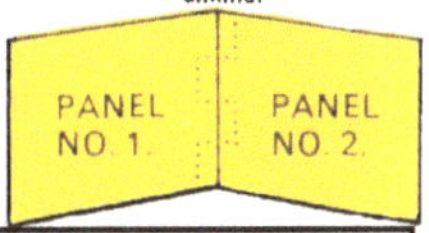

PANEL NO. 1.

PANEL NO. 2.

"FREE" Daffy Doggy "INSIDE!"
YOU GET ONE OF THESE 8 DIFFERENT "DAFFY DOGGIES" FREE INSIDE THIS PACKAGE!
COLORFUL, PLASTIC FIGURES OF SOME OF THE WILDEST...
WACKIEST, DAFFIEST DOGGIES YOU'VE EVER SEEN!
FUN TO COLLECT... FUN TO PLAY WITH AND TRADE WITH YOUR FRIENDS!
Guard Dog
Police Dog
Shepherd
Boxer
Racing Dog
Fun Dog
Guide Dog
Performing Dog
8 DIFFERENT "DAFFY DOGGIES" TO COLLECT—ONE FREE IN EACH SPECIALLY-MARKED KELLOGG'S APPLE JACKS CEREAL PACKAGE!

NEP-TUNE

and his SWITCHED —ON— SEAWEEDERS

NEP-TUNE

HAPPY HIPPY SEA HORSE

PLONKY PIANO

HARPY HARP

SAXY SALMON

SYNCOPATING SEA HORSE

FRANTIC FANNY FANTAIL

COOL CONNIE CORAL

TOM TOM TURTLE

BUBBLES BLOWFISH

SLUGSY SEA SHELL

MIKE MER-KID

OCTOPUSSY HEP-CAT

TWANGY TURTLE

FAB CRAB

Marty Monkey-wrench

Harry Hammer

Percy Pincer

Slugsy Spanner

Pat Power-drill

Georgie Grubbing Axe

Sammy Screwdriver

Paul Pliers

Henry Handbrace

Pete Penknife

Charlie Chisel

Oliver Oil-Can

Paddy Paint Brush

Muggsie Mallet

Cuthbert Chopper

Silvester Saw

Pirates & Privateers, Blackguards & Cut-throats!

Which band of these sea-going scoundrels is more evil? Some think the dreadful deeds of Roger Jolly's Pirates know no bounds. Others live in fear of Black Captain Cutlass and his crew of cut-throats. The only thing for certain is that the two are **mortal enemies!!!**

Jolly's Mealy-mouthed Men:

THE RIGHT DISHONOURABLE ROGER JOLLY, ESQ. Part-time gentleman, full-time buccaneer. Despite perfect manners and a charming personality, Jolly is one of the most bloodthirsty men ever to sail the Spanish Main.

MISTER JONATHAN GREED Obsessed with treasure, he has special responsibility for looting. Will cut a man down for a single piece of gold. Hopes to add Pierre's gold-tipped pegleg to his collection soon.

LONG THOMAS THUMBSCREW Not as gentlemanly as most of Jolly's men, he derives particular pleasure from seeing that anybody he meets promptly walks the plank and is fed to the sharks.

SIR SWASH BUCKLER Rumour has it that he gave up a life of luxury to take to piracy. The warts on his nose tell him whenever any of Captain Cutlass's men are close at hand.

Cutlass's Scurvy Crew:

BLACK CAPTAIN CUTLASS Cutlass emerged as leader of his cut-throats after proving himself to be the meanest man alive. His one burning ambition is to finish off Roger Jolly at the point of his sword.

HOOK His missing hand happened in a sword duel with Long Thomas Thumbscrew. Since then he has been obsessed with vengeance. Watch his hook-hand whatever you do.

PIERRE PEGLEG The gold tip of his pegleg makes him attractive to treasure-seekers. Lost his leg to sharks when his own Captain Cutlass had him walk the plank for mutiny. In a close knife fight he will emerge the victor.

SCARFACE Nobody knows where he came from, where his awful scars were inflicted or what secret grudges he harbours. Even his own crew trust him little.

Collect all eight, and you'll have a pirate war on your hands! Don't say you weren't warned.

Here's how the island looks. There's one half on this pack and the other half on the next Weeties pack you buy. Cut around dotted lines and stand the sections upright. Then add the extra cutouts where you think they best belong.

P.S. When you've collected one whole island, start collecting another and change its identity by using the extra cut-outs in a different way. Then you can have a double-size pirate war.

Build a Treasure Island:
Fight a Pirate War!!

ATOLL: Only room for one pirate. Complete with cannon and plenty of ammunition.

TREASURE CHEST: Coins, jewels, bullion galore. Guard it with your life. Every pirate will want to get his hands on this.

ROW BOAT: Is this the way pirates make moonlight attacks on one another's camps? Or is somebody trying to steal back to their ship unnoticed?

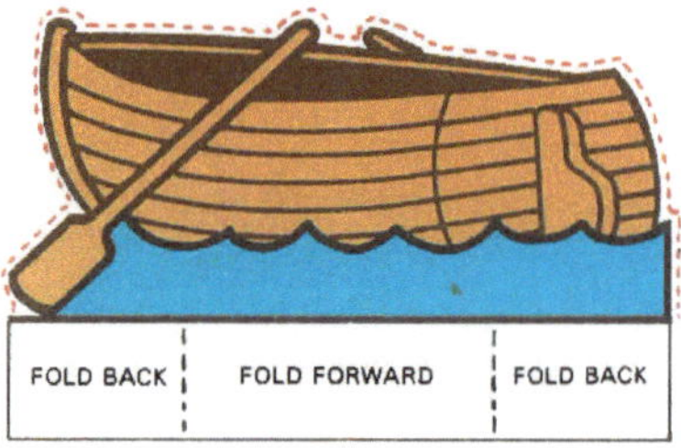

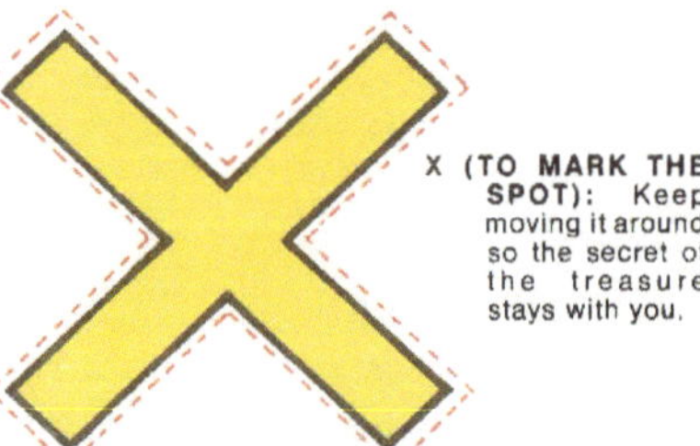

X (TO MARK THE SPOT): Keep moving it around so the secret of the treasure stays with you.

Look for Weeties pack "B" next time to complete your Treasure Island.

Build a Treasure Island: Fight a Pirate War!!

SHIP: This ship has the advantage of being able to move around. Use it to launch surprise attacks.

SKULL CAVE: A dark and forbidding place where evil things are bound to happen. Approach with caution.

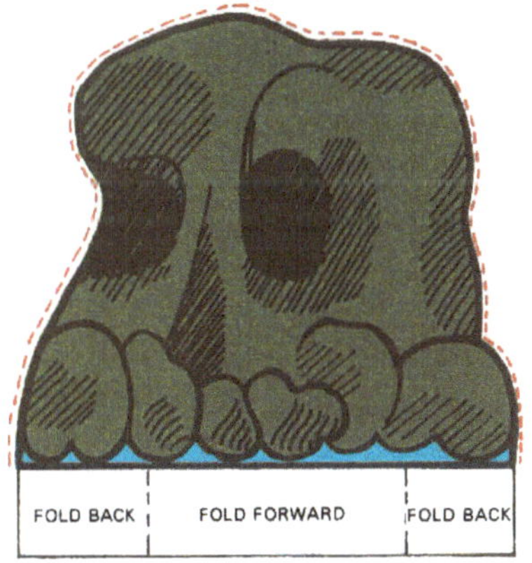

GUN EMPLACEMENT: Whichever team of pirates win this prize, they'll have a handy advantage over their enemies.

PACK B Look for Weeties pack "A" next time to complete your Treasure Island.

TOTEM-TRIBE!

BUILD YOUR OWN CRAZY 'TOTEM-POLE', PIECE BY PIECE!

How about these for real collection fun ! You can do, and make, all sorts of things with Kellogg's "Totem Tribe" people. Thread them on a string and wear them as magic charms. Put them on separate strings around the brim of your beach hat ! Build them, one on top of the other, into a colourful crazy totem pole !

There are 8 weird, and wonderful "Totem Tribe" characters for you to collect. They all have different faces, and names. You'll find one of the "Totem Tribe" in every packet of Kellogg's Corn Flakes. Look at the side panel of this packet, and see *all* the things you can do, and make with 8 of the "Totem Tribe" !

NO. 1

NO. 2

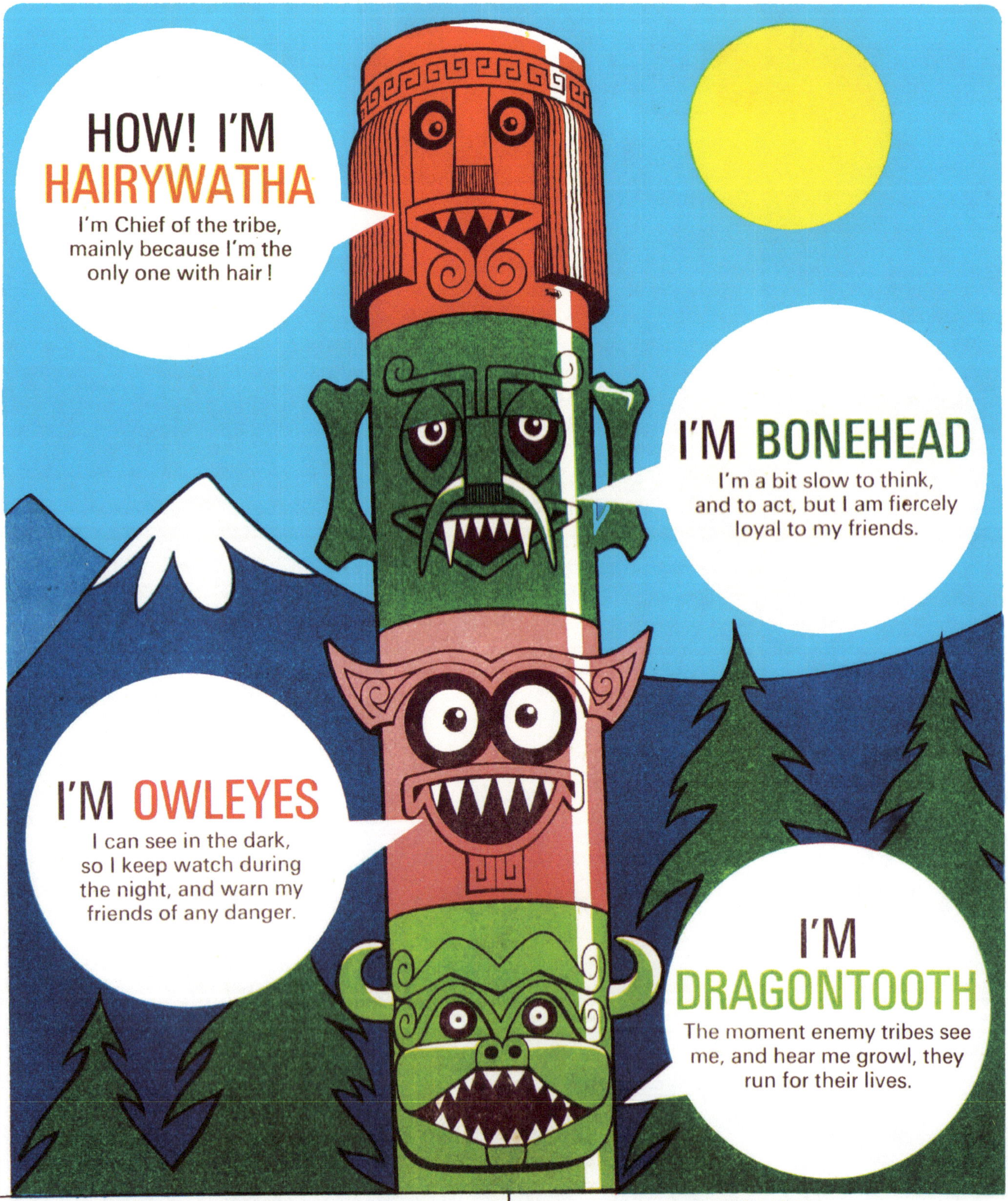

TOTEM-TRIBE!

BUILD YOUR OWN CRAZY 'TOTEM-POLE', PIECE BY PIECE!

How about these for real collection fun ! You can do, and make, all sorts of things with Kellogg's "Totem Tribe" people. Thread them on a string and wear them as magic charms. Put them on separate strings around the brim of your beach hat ! Build them, one on top of the other, into a colourful crazy totem pole !

There are 8 weird, and wonderful "Totem Tribe" characters for you to collect. They all have different faces, and names. You'll find one of the "Totem Tribe" in every packet of Kellogg's Corn Flakes. Look at the side panel of this packet, and see *all* the things you can do, and make with 8 of the "Totem Tribe" !

FLIP 'n' FEED

Just how clever are *you* at flipping a fish into the pelican's mouth? Or bananas to the monkey? Or a bone to the lion? Try your skill with Kellogg's Flip'n'Feed. It's cut-out fun, plus a plastic toy, plus a game — all in one! And most important, it is a game you can play on *your own,* or with your friends.

You'll find a 'flipper', and a different plastic food piece, in every packet of Honey Smacks*, Sugar Frosties* Froot Loops*, Lettabits*, and Strawberry Pops*. The more food pieces you collect, the more interesting the game. The rules are simple, you'll find them on the side of this packet.

*Registered Trade Marks

PANEL NO.1

30

FLIP'n'FEED

Just how clever are *you* at flipping a fish into the pelican's mouth? Or bananas to the monkey? Or a bone to the lion? Try your skill with Kellogg's Flip'n'Feed. It's cut-out fun, plus a plastic toy, plus a game — all in one! And most important, it is a game you can play on *your own*, or with your friends.

You'll find a 'flipper', and a different plastic food piece, in every packet of Honey Smacks*, Sugar Frosties* Froot Loops*, Lettabits*, and Strawberry Pops*. The more food pieces you collect, the more interesting the game. The rules are simple, you'll find them on the side of this packet.

*Registered Trade Marks

PANEL NO. 2

Kellogg's
COCO POPS
METRIC MONSTERS
Hanging five, shooting-the-tunnel, here come Kellogg's crazy ' Metric Monsters'. They clip on pencils or pens and remind you in a fun way that hertz, hectare, litre and Celsius are now part of our daily life. you'll find a ' Metric Monster' inside every packet of Kellogg's Coco Pops *, Froot Loops*, Honey Smacks *, and Frosties*.
HAIRY HECTARE
HERTZ HOG
LITRE LICKER
JULIUS CELSIUS
METRE EATER
GRABBA GRAM

Kellogg's RICE BUBBLES
thingummyjigs
HEY KIDS!
HERE COME THE THINGUMMYJIGS. Funny little creatures that look a whole lot like us people. All busy doing their own thing. Great to collect and make up your own 'Thingummyjig' society.
And because they are special people who like to go round in pairs, you will find TWO 'Thingummyjigs' in every 1 lb packet of Kellogg's * Corn Flakes, and TWO in every 1 lb and 12 oz packet of Rice Bubbles.
CHIMPY SAILOR
FISHY PELICAN
CLEVER CHICK
CROAKY DUNCE
BRAYING SWEEPER
FOXY BUTCHER
GOATY GARDENER
BRAWNY BRUIN
SHERLOCK WOLF
ARTY SQUIRREL
BIRDIE GOLFER
PORKY CHEF
ROCK ROOSTER
ADMIRAL LION
SONJA HEN
BOX A ROO
POSTIE HOUND
COCKY NEWSBOY
COWBOY QUACK-QUACK
BUNNY WAITER
*"Rice Bubbles" is a Registered Trade Mark of Kellogg (Aust) Pty. Ltd., for its delicious brand of oven-popped rice.

ZANY ZOO

SWAPPING YOUR ZANY ZOO CREATURES

When you have more than one animal, the fun begins and your animals really go crazy. Heads and tails may be swapped by snapping off and rejoining to different bodies. Legs are lots of fun because you can make a creature with four different legs by just snapping them from the four different animals! Why not go really wild and make them with heads or tails at both ends! If you want extra parts start swapping heads, legs and tails with your friends. See who amongst your friends can create the craziest creature. Now start criss-crossing their names to make up some really crazy names for your zany zoo animals.

ZANY ZOO GAME

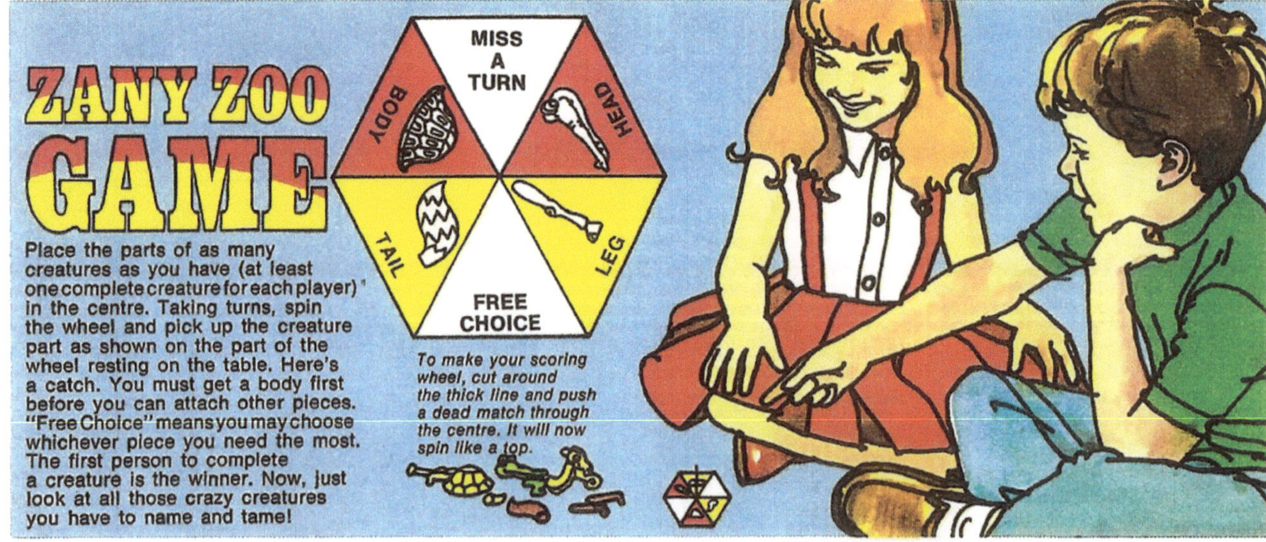

Place the parts of as many creatures as you have (at least one complete creature for each player) in the centre. Taking turns, spin the wheel and pick up the creature part as shown on the part of the wheel resting on the table. Here's a catch. You must get a body first before you can attach other pieces. "Free Choice" means you may choose whichever piece you need the most. The first person to complete a creature is the winner. Now, just look at all those crazy creatures you have to name and tame!

To make your scoring wheel, cut around the thick line and push a dead match through the centre. It will now spin like a top.

Kellogg's
RICE BUBBLES
Dingle Dangles
MAKE A DINGLE-DANGLE MOBILE
HEY KIDS! Here's a great collection for both boys and girls. Sixteen 'Dingle-Dangles' that you make up into a swaying, swinging, colourful mobile. They all have names, so if you happen to get two of the same name, swap with a friend until you have the whole dotty collection.
Kellogg's 'Dingle-Dangles' can also be worn as pendants or as a charm bracelet. Look for dotty 'Dingle-Dangles' in specially marked packets of Kellogg's Rice Bubbles.
*See the side panel for how-to-make instructions.
16 DINGLE DANGLES TO COLLECT
FLASHY FLYER
SIMON SEAHORSE
OLIVE OWL
BILLY BEE
ZIPPY ZEPPELIN
SPARROW TWIT
HARRY HELICOPTER
WILLIE WHALE
BETTY BUTTERFLY
GAY GALLEON
FANNY FISH
SAM STARFISH
GOLDIE GOLDFISH
PACIFIC PALMS
JERRY JUMPER
OCKER OCTOPUS